D1063420

SAINT
COLUMBA

SAINT
COLUMBA

EDITED AND PRESENTED
BY IAIN MACDONALD

FLORIS BOOKS

First published in 1992 by Floris Books

British Library CIP Data available

ISBN 0-86315-143-4

Printed in Great Britain
by Courier International, East Kilbride

Contents

Introduction

St Columba, otherwise known as Columcille, was born on 7 December in the year 521 into the royal clan of Conaill. He was probably born at Gartan in Country Donegal. Little is known of his early life, but it seems that he became a monk at a very early age.

Only two decades before his birth, the Gaels from Ireland had begun to colonize Argyll in the west of Scotland, while over to the east, the Angles had founded the kingdom of Bernicia. For the rest, Scotland was peopled by Picts and Britons. It appears that there was some intermingling of these peoples. The Angles and Picts were pagan, the Gaels and the Britons were Christian.

When Columba was forty-two years old, he set sail from Ireland and with twelve companions founded the Abbey of Iona, of which he was the first abbot. From there he not only established monasteries throughout Christian Scotland but also undertook the great work of converting the Picts to Christianity. He was instrumental in setting up the Gaelic kingdom of Dalriada in Argyll under its first independent king, Aidan. St Columba died in the early hours of 9 June, 597.

Adamnan was born almost thirty years after the death of Columba, and in 679 he was chosen to be the ninth abbot of Iona. Adamnan wrote the Vita Sancti Columbae *in Latin. Several copies of his work were made by hand whereby a number of textual variations occurred, and only in the last century were the extant manuscripts collated and published in Latin with a translation in English. Dr William Reeves published the Latin text in 1857. His text was based mainly on an eighth century manuscript from the monastery of Reichenau. This text was translated into English by Dr J.T. Fowler and published in 1894. It is from Fowler's English text that the extracts of this book are edited.*

Adamnan's Life of St Columba *is not so much a biography as a collection of stories about the saint. These stories are not arranged in any chronological order, but rather according to the subject matter. It is not really possible to discover a historical sequence of events. The following extracts are arranged more or less in the order in which they occur in the original.*

The Life *is divided into three books: the first tells of St Columba's prophecies, the second narrates the miracles attributed to him in his lifetime, and the third describes recorded instances of angelic manifestations.*

The life of St Columba

Adamnan's Preface

The saint's birth and early life are scantily described but a brief account of his name, his origins and his saintly destiny is given in Adamnan's Preface, where the writer also sets out his task. In undertaking the work, he is attempting not a biography as we would understand the term, but rather a collection of stories and incidents, not "doubtful and uncertain things" but "those things which have been handed down in the consistent record of our ancestors and of faithful men who knew…"

After apologizing in advance (as convention demanded) for his own "unpolished and rude" skill as a writer, Adamnan goes on to introduce his subject:

will, by God's help, first of all give some intimation concerning our abbot's name.

He was a man of venerable life and blessed memory, a father and founder of monasteries, and his name was the same as that of Jonah the prophet,… in the Latin tongue translated "Columba" (dove). It was right, therefore, that a simple and innocent man, who by his dove-like disposition made dwelling-place within himself for the Holy Spirit, should be called by this name.

Not only from the days of his infancy, but even many a year before the day of his birth, he was, as if a child of promise, named in a wonderful prophecy, the Holy Spirit revealing it to a certain soldier of Christ.

For a British holy man called Mochta, a disciple of the holy bishop, Patrick, so prophesied concerning Columba: "In the last ages of the world," he says, "a son is to be born, whose name Columba shall be spread abroad, known through all the regions of the isles of the oceans, and he shall brightly shine upon the last ages of the world..."

This prophecy, recalling prophecies of the birth of Jesus himself, was not the only sign of Columba's destiny, as Adamnan relates later:

One night, between the conception and birth of the venerable man, the angel of the Lord appeared in dreams to his mother, and let down to her, as he stood by her, a robe of wondrous beauty in which the beautiful colours as it were of all flowers appeared to be depicted, and which after a short interval he asked to have back, and took it from her hands and, lifting it up and spreading it out, let it go in the empty air.

She, being made sad by its being taken away from her, so speaks to that man of worshipful presence: "Why dost thou so soon take away from me this delightful mantle?"

He immediately replies: "For this reason, because this cloak belongs to someone of such distinguished honour, that thou wilt not be able to keep it longer with thee."

After these words, the woman saw the mantle gradually lengthening from her in its flight, and increasing in size so as to exceed the breadth of the plains, and to overtop mountains and woods in its greater measure, and she heard a voice saying:

"Woman, be not sad, for to the man to whom thou art joined in marriage thou shalt bear so famous a son, that he will be numbered with the prophets of God as one of themselves, predestined by God as the leader of innumerable souls to the celestial country."

And while she was hearing this, the woman awoke.

We are given the barest details about Columba's lineage and no account at all of his birth, upbringing and early life.

St Columba then was born of noble parentage; his father was Fedilmith, son of Fergus, his mother Aethne by name, whose father can be called in Latin Filius Navis (son of Nave), but in the Scotic (Irish) tongue Mac Nave.

In the second year after the battle of Cooladrummon, and the forty-second of his age, being desirous to make a journey for Christ from Ireland into Britain, he sailed forth.

Adamnan provides no further details of this journey across the Irish Sea which brought Columba finally to the island of Iona, where he founded his abbey and spent the last thirty-four years of his life. The writer prefers to dwell on the first abbot's saintly character and reputation:

He who from his boyhood had been devoted to the service of Christ and the study of wisdom, preserving, by the gift of God, soundness of body and purity of soul, showed that though placed upon earth he was fitted for the heavenly life. For he had as it were the face of an angel, he was polished in speech, holy in work, the best of men in disposition, great in counsel …

Not even the space of a single hour could pass by without his devoting himself to prayer, or reading or writing, or even to some manual labour. Day and night he was so engaged, without any intermission, in unwearied exercises of fasts and vigils … And meanwhile he was dear to all, ever showing a cheerful holy face, and was gladdened in his inmost heart by the joy of the Holy Spirit.

I Prophetic revelations

The following extracts from Book I give evidence of the saint's remarkable prophetic powers. But not only did Columba prophesy the future, on a scale ranging from great political events to minor and apparently trivial happenings; he also had the power of far-vision, that is the ability to "see" contemporary events happening at a great distance.

A prophecy concerning Ernene

At another time the blessed man, while staying some months in the central part of Ireland, founding by divine favour his monastery, which is called in the Irish language Dairmag (Durrow), thought it well to visit the brethren who were dwelling together in St Kiaran's monastery at Clonmacnoise. And on hearing of his arrival, every one from the fields about the monastery, together with those who were found gathered together within it, following with all eagerness their abbot Alither, set off with one consent, going outside the enclosure of the monastery, to meet St Columba, as an angel of the Lord. And they humbly bowed with their faces to the earth as they saw him, and with all reverence they kissed him, and raising their voices in hymns and praises, they conducted him through with all honour to the church. And, tying together a canopy or barrier of poles, they had it borne by four men walking in pairs around the saint as he walked, lest a man of St Columba's age should be thronged by the crowding together of such a multitude of the brethren.

And in that same hour a certain servant-boy, much cast down in countenance and meanly clad, and not yet approved by his elders, came behind, hiding himself as much as he could, that he might touch even the fringe of that cloak which the blessed man wore, secretly, and if possible without his knowing or perceiving it. But yet this was not hidden from the saint, for that which with his bodily eyes he could not see done behind him he perceived by spiritual vision. And so he suddenly stops, stretches out his hand behind him, catches the boy by the neck, and, drawing him forth, sets him in front of him, while all those who are standing around say: "Send him away! Send him away! Why dost thou detain this wretched and troublesome boy?"

But the saint, on the other hand, utters these prophetic words from his pure heart: "Suffer it to be so now, brethren; suffer it to be so now." But to the boy, who is trembling all over, he says: "O my son, open thy mouth, and put out thy tongue."

Then the boy at his bidding, and with much trembling, opened his mouth and put out his tongue, and the saint, stretching forth his holy hand, earnestly blesses it, and thus prophetically speaks, saying: "Although this boy may now appear to you as one to be despised and of very low estate, yet let no one despise him on that account. For from this hour not only will he not displease you, but he will greatly please you, and in good conduct and the virtues of the soul he will by degrees advance from day to day; wisdom also and prudence shall from this day be increased in him more and more, and great is his future career in this your congregation; his tongue also shall be endued by God with wholesome doctrine and eloquence."

This was Ernene, son of Crasene, afterwards

famous and of the greatest note among all the churches of Scotia [Ireland].

Prophecy concerning the sons of King Aidan
At another time, the saint questions King Aidan respecting his successor in the kingdom. On his replying that he does not know which of his three sons is to reign, whether Artur, or Eochoid Find, or Domingart, the saint straightway prophesies on this wise: "Not one of these three will be ruler, for they will fall in battles, being destined to be slain by their enemies; but now, if thou hast any younger sons, let them come to me, and the one whom God will choose out of them as king will suddenly rush on to my lap."

And when they were called in, Eochoid Buide, according to the word of the saint, came to him and lay in his bosom. And immediately the saint kissed him, and blessed him, and says to his father: "This is the survivor, and is to reign king after thee, and his sons will reign after him."

And so all things were afterwards completely fulfilled in their seasons. For Artur and Eochoid Find were slain, no long time after, in the battle of the Miathi; Domingart was slain in Saxonia

(England) in the carnage of battle; but Eochoid
Buide succeeded to the kingdom after his father.

How the saint knew beforehand of a great whale
On a certain day, while the venerable man was
living in Iona, one of the brethren, Berachus by
name, proposing to sail to the Ethican island
(Tiree), came to the saint in the morning and
asked his blessing.

And the saint looked upon him and said: "O
my son, take great care today not to attempt to
cross over in a direct course to the Ethican land
by the wider sea, but rather go round about and
sail by the smaller islands, lest terrified by some
monstrous prodigy, thou shouldst scarcely be
able to escape thence."

He, having received a blessing from the saint,
departed, got on board the ship and set off, as if
lightly regarding the word of the saint. And
thereupon, in passing over the wider reaches of
the Ethican sea, he and the sailors who were
with him look, and, behold, a whale of wondrous and immense size, lifting itself up like a
mountain, while, floating on the surface, it
opened wide its yawning mouth, all bristling
with teeth.

Then the rowers let down the sail, terribly

alarmed, and, turning back, could scarcely escape from that tumult of the waves which arose from the motion of the monster, and, calling to mind the prophetic saying of the saint, they greatly marvelled.

The same day also, the saint gave an intimation in the morning to Baithene, who was about to sail to the above-mentioned island, concerning the same whale, saying: "In the middle of this last night a great whale has come up from the depths of the sea, and today it will lift itself up upon the surface of the ocean, between the Iouan and the Ethican islands."

Baithene answers him and says: "That monster and I are under the power of God."

Then says the saint: "Go in peace, thy faith in Christ shall defend thee from this danger."

So Baithene, having received a blessing from the saint, sails out from the port, and as soon as he and his companions have crossed over considerable reaches of sea, they behold the whale, and while all the rest are terribly alarmed, he alone is bold, and with both his hands upraised he blesses the sea and the whale. And in that very moment the huge monster dived under the waves, and nowhere appeared to them again.

Of the vowel letter "I"

One day Baithene comes up to the saint, and says: "I must have one of the brethren to run over with me and correct the Psalter which I have written."

On hearing which the saint thus speaks: "Why do you bring this trouble upon us without any occasion? For in this thy Psalter of which thou speakest there will not be found one letter over much nor another wanting, except the vowel *i,* which alone is wanting."

And so, when the whole Psalter had been read through, it was found on examination that what the saint had said was true.

Of a book that fell into a water-vessel, as the saint had predicted

One day again, while sitting at the hearth in the monastery, he sees Lugbe, of the tribe Mocumin, reading a book at a distance, to whom he suddenly says: "Take care, my son, take care; for I think that the book which thou art reading is going to fall into a vessel full of water."

Which soon so happened, for that youth above mentioned, after some short time, rose to attend to something in the monastery, and forgot the word of the blessed man, so the book, which he carelessly held under his arm, suddenly fell into the vessel full of water.

Concerning a city burnt by fire from heaven
At another time again, Lugbe, of the tribe Mocumin, of whom we have made mention above, came one day to the saint after the grinding of corn, and could in no wise look upon his face, overspread as it was with a wonderful flush; and being greatly alarmed he quickly fled.

But the saint, gently clapping his hands, calls him back. And being asked by the saint immediately on his return why he had fled so fast, he gave this reply: "I fled because I was very much afraid."

And after some little time, acting with more confidence, he ventures to question the saint, saying: "Has any awful vision been manifested unto thee in this hour?"

The saint made answer thus to him: "So terrible a vengeance has now been wrought in a remote portion of the globe."

"What manner of vengeance?" says the youth, "and in what region wrought?"

Then the saint thus speaks: "A sulphureous flame has in this hour been poured from heaven

over a city of Roman jurisdiction within the
boundaries of Italy, and nearly three thousand
men, women and children, have perished. And
before the present year is over, Gallic sailors,
arriving from the provinces of the Gauls, will
relate these same things to thee."

Which words were after some months proved
to have been true sayings. For the same Lugbe,
going in company with the holy man to the
Land's Head (Kintyre), questioning the captain
and sailors of a bark that arrived, hears narrated
by them all those things about the city with its
citizens, as they were predicted by the illustrious
man.

Of a certain rich man named Lugud Clodus
At another time, while the saint was staying in
Scotia for some days, he saw another clerk
mounted on a chariot, and gaily driving over the
plain of Bregh in Meath. First asking about him
who he was, he received this answer concerning
him from the man's friends: "This is Lugud
Clodus, a man who is rich, and honoured
among the people."

The saint thereupon answers and says: "I do
not so regard him, but rather as a poor wretched
creature who on the day of his death will be

retaining at his place in one enclosure three stray cattle of his neighbours; and of these strays he will order one selected cow to be killed for himself, and will ask for some part of her cooked flesh to be given to him, while he is lying in the same bed with a harlot. And as soon as he takes a bite out of that portion, he will be choked there and then, and will die."

All which things, as is related by well-informed persons, were fulfilled according to the prophetic word of the saint.

Of Cronan, a bishop

At another time, a certain stranger came to the saint from the province of the Munster-men, and in his humility disguised himself as much as he could, that no one might know he was a bishop, but yet this could not be hidden from the saint. For on one Lord's day, being requested by the saint to prepare Christ's Body according to custom, he calls the saint to him, that they may break the Lord's Bread together, as two presbyters.

The saint thereupon goes up to the altar, and, suddenly looking on his face, thus addresses him: "Christ bless thee, brother; break this bread alone, by the episcopal rite; now we know that thou art a bishop. Wherefore hast thou thus far tried to disguise thyself, so that the veneration due to thee was not rendered unto thee by us?"

On hearing this discourse of the saint, the humble stranger, greatly astonished, worshipped Christ in the holy man, and those who were present, greatly wondering, glorified the Lord.

Concerning a crane that flew to the shore
For, indeed, at another time, when the saint was living in Iona, he calls one of the brethren to him, and thus addresses him: "On the third day from this that is breaking, thou oughtest to sit on the sea-shore, and look out in the western part of this island; for from the northern part of Ireland, a certain guest, a crane to wit, beaten by the winds during long and circuitous aerial flights, will arrive after the ninth hour of the day, very weary and fatigued, and, its strength being almost gone, it will fall down before thee and lie on the beach. Thou wilt take care to lift it up tenderly, and carry it to some neighbouring house; and, while it is there hospitably received, thou wilt diligently feed it, attending to it for three days and three nights; and then, refreshed after the three days are fulfilled, and unwilling to

sojourn any longer with us, it will return with fully recovered strength to its former sweet home in Scotia whence it came; and I so earnestly commend it to thee, because it comes from our fatherland."

The brother obeys, and on the third day, after the ninth hour, as he had been bidden, he awaits the coming of the anticipated guest, and then, when it is come; fallen, he lifts it from the beach; weak, he bears it to the hospice; hungry, he feeds it. And when he has returned to the monastery in the evening, the saint, not questioning, but declaring, says: "God bless thee, my son, for that thou hast well attended to our stranger guest, which will not tarry long in its wanderings, but after three days will return to its native land."

Which the event also proved, just as the saint predicted. For after being lodged for three days, it first lifted itself up on high by flying from the earth in the presence of its ministering host; then, after looking out its way in the air for a little while, it crossed the ocean wave, and returned to Ireland in a straight course of flight on a calm day.

II Miracles

We come now to Book II which tells of the wonderful miracles performed by St Columba and notably of his healing powers and his control of the winds and storms. There are resemblances again to the miracles performed by Jesus as related in the gospels. Remarkable, too, is St Columba's ban on serpents on the isle of Iona which holds good till our day and which he prophesied would continue as long as there was Christian worship on the island. Worthy of note, as well, is Columba's encounter with the Loch Ness monster!

Of the wine made out of water

At another time, when the venerable man was staying in Scotia with St Findbar (Finnian) the bishop, while he was yet a youth, learning the wisdom of Holy Scripture, on a certain solemn day the wine for the sacrificial mystery, by some chance, was not found. And when he heard the ministers of the altar complaining among themselves of the want of it, he, as deacon, takes a pitcher and goes to the spring, to draw spring water for the ministrations of the Holy Eucharist, for in those days he was ministering in the order of the diaconate.

And so the blessed man in faith blessed the watery element which he drew from the spring, calling on the name of the Lord Jesus Christ, who in Cana of Galilee turned water into wine, who also working in this miracle, the inferior, that is, the watery nature, was by the hands of the famous man converted into the more agreeable species, that namely of wine.

And so the holy man, returning from the spring and entering the church, places by the altar the pitcher having within it such liquid; and says to the ministers: "Ye have wine, which the Lord Jesus has sent for the execution of His mysteries."

When they understood this, the holy bishop with the ministers together give great thanks to God. But the holy youth ascribed this not to himself, but to the holy bishop Findbar. And so Christ the Lord manifested this first proof of power by His disciple, which He wrought by Himself in the same case, placing it as the beginning of miracles in Cana of Galilee.

Of the holy virgin Maugina, daughter of Daimen
At another time the saint, while he was living in
Iona, at the first hour of the day calls to him a
certain brother, Lugaid by name, whose sur-
name in the Irish language is Lathir, and thus
addresses him, saying: "Make ready quickly for
a hasty voyage to Scotia, for it is very necessary
for me to send thee as a messenger to Clocher of
the sons of Daimen. For in his last night
Maugina, a holy virgin, a daughter of Daimen,
returning home from the oratory after Vespers,
by some chance has taken a false step, and her
hip is broken in twain. This woman in her cries
is often calling my name to remembrance,
hoping that through me she will receive comfort
from the Lord."

As Lugaid is obeying, and straightway setting
out, the saint hands to him a little box of
pine-wood containing a blessed gift, saying:
"Let the blessed gift contained in this little box,
when thou comest to visit Maugina, be put into
a vessel of water, and let the same water of
blessing be poured over her hip; and immediately, on calling upon the name of God, the
hip-bone will be joined and united, and the holy
virgin will recover perfect health."

And the saint adds these words: "Behold! I do

now in person write in the cover of this box the number of twenty-three years, during which the holy virgin is to live in this present life after the same cure."

All which things were thus completely fulfilled, as predicted by the saint; for, as soon as Lugaid came to the holy virgin, and her hip was bathed, as the saint recommended, with the blessed water, the bone was united without any, even the least, delay, and she was completely cured; and, rejoicing in the coming of the messenger of St Columba with great thanksgiving, lived, according to the prophecy of the saint, for twenty-three years after her cure, continuing in good works.

Of a spring of malignant water

At another time, the blessed man, while he was sojourning in the province of the Picts for some days, heard among the heathen people that a report was spread abroad concerning a spring which senseless men, the devil blinding their understanding, worshipped as a god. For those who drank of the same spring, or purposely washed their hands or feet in it, being by God's permission smitten by demoniacal artifice, returned either leprous or purblind, or certainly weak, or attacked by some other maladies, on account of all which things the heathen men were led astray, and rendered divine honour to the spring.

On finding that these things were so, the saint one day went boldly up to the spring at the sight of which the Druids, whom he himself had often sent away confounded and vanquished by him, greatly rejoiced, thinking indeed that he would suffer similar things from the touch of that noxious water.

But he, first lifting up his holy hand, with invocation of the Name of Christ, washes his hands and feet, and then, together with his companions, drinks of the same water that had been blessed by him. And from that day the demons departed from the spring; and not only was it not permitted to injure anyone but even, after the blessing of the saint and his washing therein, many diseases among the people were healed by the same spring.

Of the danger of the blessed man on the sea
At another time, the holy man began to be in peril by the sea, for the entire hull of the ship was heavily struck, and violently dashed about

on the huge mountains of the waves, while a great tempest of winds bore upon them on every side.

Then by chance the sailors say to the saint as he is endeavouring with them to empty the bilges: "What thou now doest doth not greatly profit us in our danger; thou shouldst rather pray for us now that we are perishing."

On hearing which, he ceases to empty out the bitter water, the green sea-wave, but begins to pour out sweet and earnest prayer to the Lord. Wondrous to say, in the same moment of time in which the saint, standing at the prow with his hands stretched out to heaven, besought the Almighty, the whole storm of wind and the raging of the sea, being stilled more quickly than can be said, ceased, and at once there followed a most tranquil calm. But they who were in the ship were amazed, and, rendering thanks with great wonder, glorified the Lord in the holy and famous man.

Of another similar peril to him by the sea

At another time again, when a cruel and dangerous tempest was pressing heavily on them, and his companions were crying out for the saint to beseech the Lord for them, he gave them this answer, saying: "On this day it is not my lot to pray for you who are placed in this danger, but it is that of the abbot Cainnech, a holy man."

I am going to relate wonderful things. At that same hour St Cainnech, living in his monastery, which in Latin is called Campulus Bovis, but in the Irish language Ached-bou (Aghaboe), the Holy Spirit revealing it to him, heard with the inward ear of his heart the above-mentioned saying of St Columba; and when by chance he had begun after the ninth hour to break the holy-bread in the refectory, he quickly leaves the table, and, with one shoe clinging to his foot, while in his great haste the other was left behind, he hurriedly makes his way to the church, saying as he goes: "It is not for us to dine now, at a time when the ship of St Columba is in peril by the sea. For even now is he frequently calling on the name of this Cainnech, that he may pray Christ for him and his companions in peril."

Entering the oratory after these his words, he prayed for a little while on bended knees, and, the Lord hearing his prayer, the tempest straightway ceased, and the sea became very tranquil. Then St Columba, seeing in spirit

Cainnech's hastening to the church, although he was living so far away, wonderfully utters this sentence from his pure breast, saying: "Now I know, O Cainnech, that God hath heard thy prayer, now doth thy rapid race to the church with one shoe greatly profit us."

In such a miracle as this, the prayer of both holy men, as we believe, had a joint effect.

Of the staff of St Cainnech, forgotten at the harbour

At another time, the same Cainnech who is mentioned above, when beginning to sail from the harbour of Iona to Scotia, forgot to take his staff with him; which staff of his, indeed, being found on the shore after his departure, was put into the hand of St Columba, and which, on his return home, he carries into the oratory, and there he remains some time alone in prayer.

Cainnech then approaching the Oidechan island (Islay?), suddenly pricked to the heart for his forgetfulness, was inwardly cast down. But after some little time he got down from the ship, and, kneeling down in prayer on the land, found in front of him, upon the turf of the little land of Aithche, the staff which he had forgotten and left behind him at the harbour of Iona island. At its being thus carried out for him by the agency of divine power, he greatly marvelled, with giving of thanks in God.

Of fishes specially prepared by God

At another time, when some companions of the famous man, keen fishermen, had taken five fishes in a net in the fishful river Sale, the saint says to them: "Cast your net a second time into the river, and immediately you will find a great fish, which the Lord hath prepared for me."

They, obeying the word of the saint, drew forth in the net a salmon of wondrous size prepared for him by God.

At another time again, while the saint was staying for some days near Lough Ce (Key), he stopped his companions when they wanted to go fishing, saying: "Today and tomorrow not a fish will be found in the river; I will send you on the third day, and you will find two great river salmon caught in the net."

And so they, after two days, casting the net, drew to the land two fish of most unusual size, which they found in the river called Bo (Boyle). In these two fishings that have been mentioned, the power of miracle appears, together with prophetic foreknowledge accompanying it; for

which things the saint and his companions
rendered special thanks to God.

Of the death of evil-doers

The venerable man greatly loved Columban,
whom the virtue of his benediction made rich
from having been a poor man, because he
rendered to him many offices of kindness. Now
there was at that time a certain man, an
evil-doer, a persecutor of good men, named
Ioan son of Conall son of Domhnall, sprung of
the royal race of Gabhran. This man persecuted
the above-mentioned Columban, the friend of
St Columba, and laid waste his homestead,
carrying off everything that could be found
therein, acting in this hostile fashion not once
only, but twice.

Whence by chance it happened, and not
undeservedly, to that evil-natured man, that on
a third occasion, after a third harrying of that
same homestead, while returning laden with
spoil to the ship, together with his comrades, he
had, straight before him, drawing nearer to him,
the blessed man whom he had, as it were,
despised at a distance. And when the saint
reproved him for his evil deeds, and would
persuade him, begging him to lay down the

spoil, he, remaining savage and not to be
persuaded, despised the saint, and getting on
board the ship with the spoil, scoffed at the
blessed man, and laughed him to scorn.

But the saint followed him even to the sea,
and walking into the glassy sea-waters up to the
knees, with both hands lifted up to heaven he
earnestly prays to Christ, who glorifies His
chosen ones that glorify Him. Now that harbour, in which he stood and prayed to the Lord
for some little while after the persecutor had
sailed out, is in the place which in the Irish
language is called Ait-Chambas Art-muirchol
(Camus-an-Gaal, Ardnamurchan). Then the
saint, when he had finished his prayer and
returned to the dry land, sits down in a more
elevated place with his companions, to whom in
that hour he utters these very terrible words,
saying: "This wretched creature, who hath
despised Christ in His servants, will never
return to the harbour from which he hath lately
gone out in your presence; but neither will he
arrive with his companions in evil-doing at
other lands which he seeks, being prevented by
sudden death. Today will the fierce storm,
which you will soon see arising out of a cloud on
the north, be hurled against and drown him

with his companions, nor will even one of them remain to tell the tale."

After waiting a very little while, on a most calm day, behold then the cloud rising from the sea, as the saint had said, sent forth with mighty crash of wind, and finding the robber with his spoil between the Malean and Colosan islands (Mull and Colonsay), drowned him in the midst of the sea so suddenly lashed into fury; nor, according to the word of the saint, did even one of those who had been in the ship escape; and in a wonderful manner, while on every side the whole of the sea remained calm, did such a single storm cast down to hell the robbers that were drowned miserably indeed, but deservedly.

Of the driving away of a certain water monster
At another time again, when the blessed man was staying for some days in the province of the Picts, he found it necessary to cross the river Ness; and, when he came to the bank thereof, he sees some of the inhabitants burying a poor unfortunate little fellow, whom, as those who were burying him reported, some water monster had a little before snatched at as he was

swimming, and bitten with a most savage bite,
and whose hapless corpse some men who came
in a boat to give assistance, though too late,
caught hold of by putting out hooks.

The blessed man however, on hearing this,
directs that some one of his companions shall
swim out and bring to him the coble that is on
the other bank, sailing it across. On hearing this
direction of the holy and famous man, Lugne
Mocumin, obeying without delay, throws off
all his clothes except his undergarment, and
casts himself into the water.

Now the monster, which before was not so
much satiated as made eager for prey, was lying
hid in the bottom of the river; but perceiving
that the water above was disturbed by him who
was crossing, suddenly emerged, and, swimming to the man as he was crossing in the
middle of the stream, rushed up with a great
roar and open mouth.

Then the blessed man looked on, while all
who were there, as well the heathen as even the
brethren, were stricken with very great terror;
and, with his holy hand raised on high, he
formed the saving sign of the cross in the empty
air, invoked the Name of God, and commanded
the fierce monster, saying: "Think not to go

further, nor touch thou the man. Quick! go back!"

Then the beast, on hearing this voice of the saint, was terrified and fled backward more rapidly than he came, as if dragged by cords, although before it had come so near to Lugne as he swam, that there was not more than the length of one punt-pole between the man and the beast. Then the brethren, seeing that the beast had gone away, and that their comrade Lugne was returned to them safe and sound in the boat, glorified God in the blessed man, greatly marvelling. Moreover also the barbarous heathens who were there present, constrained by the greatness of that miracle, which they themselves had seen, magnified the God of the Christians.

Of the land of this island, Iona, blessed by the One day of the same summertime in which he departed to the Lord, the saint goes, borne in a wagon, to visit the brethren who were engaged in heavy work in the western plain of Iona. After some consolatory addresses spoken to them by the saint, he, standing on a more elevated spot, thus prophesies, saying: "From this day, my sons, I know that you will never for the future be able to see my face again in the places on this plain."

And seeing them greatly saddened on hearing this saying, and endeavouring to console them as much as might be, he lifts up both his holy hands, and, blessing the whole of this our island, says: "From this hour's space, the poisons of no vipers shall in any wise be able to hurt either men or cattle in the lands of this island, so long as the inhabitants of this same place of our sojourning observe the commands of Christ."

Of one Lugne, a pilot

At another time, while the saint was being entertained in the Rechrean island, a certain countryman came to him and complained about his wife, who, as he said, had taken a dislike to him, and would in no wise allow him to come near her for marriage rights.

On hearing this, the saint called the wife to him, and, so far as he could, began to reprove her on that account, saying: "Wherefore, woman, dost thou endeavour to repel from thee thine own flesh, when the Lord saith, *They twain shall be in one flesh?* Therefore the flesh of thy husband is thine own flesh."

She answers and says: "All things whatsoever

thou shalt enjoin to me, though they be ever so severe, I am prepared to fulfil, one thing only excepted, that in no wise thou constrain me to sleep in one bed with Lugne. I do not refuse to undertake all the management of the house; or, if thou biddest, even to cross the seas, and remain in some monastery of maidens."

The saint then says: "That which thou sayest cannot be rightly done, for thou art bound by the law of a husband so long as the husband liveth. For it would be a sin for those whom God hath lawfully joined to be put asunder."

And, having thus spoken, he next added: "In this day three persons, that is, I and the husband, with the wife, will pray unto the Lord, fasting."

Hereupon she says: "I know that to thee it will not be impossible that those things which appear to be difficult, or even impossible, may be granted, when sought of God."

The wife the same day agrees to fast with the saint, prayed for them, taking no sleep; and on the next day the saint, in the husband's presence, thus addresses the wife: "O woman, art thou prepared today, as thou wast saying yesterday, to go out to a monastery of women?"

She says: "Now I know that thy prayer concerning me is heard by God, for the man whom yesterday I disliked today I love; for during this last night my heart, how I know not, has been changed in me from dislike to love."

Why make a long story? From that same day to the day of her death the soul of this wife was indissolubly cemented in love of her husband, so that in no way did she thenceforth deny those rights of marriage which before she refused to render.

III Angelic visitations

Book III tells us of the angels seen on various significant occasions, beginning with the visitation to Columba's mother before his birth (see Preface). Book III concludes with the very moving account of St Columba's death and the vision of angels that accompanied his passing away.

Of angels conducting the soul of one Diormit to heaven

t another time, a certain Irish stranger came to the saint, and abode with him for some months in Iona. One day the blessed man says to him: "Now is one of the clergy of thy province, whose name I do not yet know, being carried to heaven by angels."

But the brother, on hearing this, began to search within himself about the province of the Anteriores (Easterns), who in the Irish language are named Indairthir (men of East Oriel, in Ulster), and about the name of that blessed man;

and then made this remark, saying: "I know another soldier of Christ, named Diormit, who built for himself a small monastery in the same district wherein I also was living."

The saint says to him: "He it is of whom thou art speaking, who has now been conducted into Paradise by the angels of God."

But this also must very carefully be noted, that there were many secrets, holy mysteries, revealed to him by God, but concealed from others, which the same venerable man in no wise suffered to be brought to the knowledge of men; there being two reasons for this, as he himself once hinted to a few brethren, namely, that he might avoid vainglory, and, that he might not encourage, for the purpose of asking questions of himself, intolerable crowds of persons wishing to make inquiries concerning him, when the fame of his revelations was spread abroad.

Of an apparition of holy angels meeting the soul of blessed Brendan

Another day in like manner, while the venerable man was living in Iona, early in the morning he calls to him his oft-mentioned attendant, Diormit by name, and gives him directions, saying:

"Let the sacred ministrations of the Eucharist be quickly prepared. For today is the festival of blessed Brendan."

"Wherefore," says the attendant, "dost thou direct that such solemnities of masses be prepared on this day, for no messenger of the death of that holy man has come to us from Scotia?"

"Go," then says the saint, "thou oughtest to obey my direction. For this last night I saw the heaven suddenly opened, and choirs of angels descending to meet the soul of the holy Brendan; by whose luminous and incomparable brightness the whole compass of the world was enlightened in that hour."

Of a multitude of angels seen descending

At another time again, the blessed man one day, while living in Iona, the brethren being gathered together, charged them with great earnestness, saying to them: "Today I desire to go out alone into the western plain of our island; therefore let none of you follow me."

And on their professing obedience, he goes out alone, as he wished. But a certain brother, a crafty, prying fellow, slipping off another way, secretly ensconces himself in the top of a certain little hill which overlooks the same plain;

desiring, you see, to find out the cause of that solitary expedition of the blessed man.

And when the same spy, from the top of the hillock, beheld him standing on a certain little hill on that plain, praying with his hands spread out to heaven, and lifting up his eyes to heaven; wonderful to say, behold then suddenly a marvellous sight appeared, which the same above-mentioned man, as I think, not without the permission of God, saw even with bodily eyes, from his place on the little hill; that the name of the saint, and the honour due to him, might afterwards, though against his own will, be the more spread abroad among the people on account of this vision thus vouchsafed.

For holy angels, citizens of the celestial country, flying to him with wonderful swiftness, and clothed in white robes, began to stand around the holy man as he prayed; and, after some conversation with the blessed man, that heavenly host, as if perceiving itself to be under observation, quickly sped back to the highest heavens. And the blessed man himself, after the angelic conference, on his return to the monastery, again gathers the brethren together, and with no ordinary chiding inquires which of them is guilty of transgression.

And, when they then declare that they do not know, the offender, conscious of his inexcusable transgression, and not enduring further to conceal his fault, on bended knees, in the midst of the choir of the brethren, as a suppliant, begs pardon before the saint. The saint, leading him aside, charges him, with severe threatening, as he kneels before him, that to no man must he disclose anything, not even a little secret, concerning that angelic vision, during the life of the same blessed man.

But after the departure of the holy man from the body, he related that apparition of the heavenly host to the brethren, with solemn attestation. Whence, even to this day, the place of that angelic conference attests the event that took place there by its own proper name, which in Latin can be rendered Colliculus Angelorum; but in the Irish language Cnoc Angel (the Angels' hill, now Sithean Mor, the greater Fairies' hill).

Wherefore we must direct our thoughts, and very carefully examine, how great and of what nature were those sweet visits of angels to the blessed man, for the most part in winter nights, as he was watching and praying in the more secret places, while others slept; visits which could in no way come to the knowledge of men, and no doubt were very numerous. And even if some of them could in any way be found out by men, whether by day or by night, these without a doubt were very few in comparison with those angelic visits which could be known by no one. This also is in like manner to be noted concerning some luminous manifestations, which were found out by a few persons, and will be described below.

Of the descent or visitation of the Holy Spirit
At another time, while the holy man was sojourning in Hinba island, the grace of holy inspiration was poured out upon him in an abundant and incomparable manner, and wonderfully continued with him for three days; so that, for three days and as many nights, he remained within a house which was locked up and filled with celestial light, would suffer no man to come near him, and neither did eat nor drink.

And from this house, rays of intense brightness were seen at night, breaking out through the chinks of the doors and the keyholes. Some spiritual songs also, which had not been heard before, were then heard as they were being sung by him.

But he himself also, as he afterwards declared before a very few persons, saw, openly manifested, many secret things, hidden ever since the foundation of the world. Some obscure and most difficult passages of the sacred Scriptures appeared plain; and in that light were more clearly manifested to the eyes of his most pure heart. He lamented that Baithene his foster-son was not present; had he chanced to be there in those three days, he might have written down many things from the lips of the blessed man; mysteries unknown by other men, either concerning past ages, or those which were next to follow; and also some explanations of the sacred volumes. Baithene however could not be present, being detained by contrary winds in the Egean island (Eigg) until those three days and as many nights of that incomparable and glorious visitation came to a close.

Of the passing away to the Lord of our holy patron Columba

The holy man, as a true prophet, knew long beforehand, the term of his present life was to be completed; one day in the month of May, the old man, borne in a wagon, being feeble with age, goes to visit the working brethren. To whom, while at their labours in the western part of Iona, on that day he began to speak thus, saying: "During the Paschal solemnity in the month of April past, with desire I desired to pass away to Christ the Lord; as indeed had been granted me by Him, if I had preferred it. But, lest your festival of gladness should be turned into sorrow, I chose rather that the day of my departure out of the world should be put off a little longer."

The monks of his household, when they heard from him these mournful tidings, were greatly distressed, and he began to cheer them, so far as in him lay, with words of consolation. Which being ended, as he was sitting in the carriage, he turned his face to the east, and blessed the island with the dwellers in that island home; from which day, as has been written above, the poisons of the three-cleft tongues of vipers even to this day have not been able in any way to hurt either man or beast. After those words of benediction the saint was carried back to his monastery.

Then, in the course of a few days, while the solemnities of masses were being celebrated, according to custom, on the Lord's day; all on a sudden the face of the venerable man, as his eyes are lifted upward, is seen suffused with a ruddy glow, for, as it is written, *When the heart is glad the face blooms.* For in that same hour he alone saw an angel of the Lord hovering above within the walls of his oratory. And, because the lovely and tranquil aspect of the holy angels pours joy and gladness into the hearts of the elect, this was the cause of that sudden gladness imparted to the blessed man.

And when those who were therein present inquired as to what was the cause of the joy that was kindled within him, the saint, looking upward, gave them this reply: "Wonderful and incomparable is the subtlety of the nature of angels. For, behold, an angel of the Lord, sent to demand some deposit dear to God, looking down from above upon us within the church, and blessing us, has returned again through the vaulting of the church, and has left no traces of such an exit."

So far the saint. But yet, as to the nature of that deposit for which the angel was sent to make inquiry, not one of those who were standing around was able to form an opinion. Our patron, however, gave the name of a holy

deposit to his own soul, which had been
entrusted to him by God; which soul, as will be
narrated below, in the night of the next Lord's
day, six days in succession coming between,
passed away to the Lord.

And so the venerable man at the end of the
same week, that is on the Sabbath day (Satur-
day), himself and his dutiful attendant Diormit,
go to bless the granary, which was close at hand.
On entering which, when he blessed both it and
two heaps of corn that were stored therein, he
uttered these words with giving of thanks,
saying: "I greatly congratulate the monks of my
household that this year also, if I should have to
depart from you to any place, ye will have
enough for the year."

On hearing this saying, Diormit his attendant
began to be sorrowful, and to speak thus: "In the
course of this year, Father, thou art often
making us sorrowful, because thou so frequently makest mention of thy departure."

To whom the saint gave this reply: "I have
some little secret discourse, and if thou wilt
faithfully promise me not to disclose it to any
one before my death, I shall be able to give thee
some clearer intimation concerning my departure."

When the attendant, on bended knees, had made his promise, according to the wish of the saint, the venerable man thus speaks: "This day is in the sacred volumes called Sabbath, which is, being interpreted, Rest. And for me this day is a Sabbath indeed, because it is the last day of this my present laborious life, in which I take my rest after all the wearinesses of my labours. And in the middle of this most solemn eve of the Lord's day that is now coming, according to the saying of the Scriptures, *I shall go the way of my fathers.* For even now my Lord Jesus Christ deigneth to invite me, to Whom, I say, in the middle of this night, I shall depart, at His invitation. For thus it hath been revealed unto me by the Lord Himself."

The attendant on hearing these sad words began to weep bitterly, but the saint endeavoured to console him as well as he could.

After this, the saint goes out of the granary, and, returning to the monastery, sits down at the half-way place where a cross, afterwards fixed in a millstone, and still standing at this day, is to be seen on the side of the road. And while the saint, feeble with age, as I said before, sat down for a little while and rested in that place, behold! there comes up to him the white horse, that faithful servant that used to carry the milk-pails between the cowshed and the monastery. This creature then coming up to the saint, wonderful to say, putting its head in his bosom, as I believe under the inspiration of God, in Whose sight every animal is endowed with a sense of things, because the Creator Himself hath so ordered it; knowing that his master would soon depart from him, and that he would see his face no more, began to utter plaintive moans, and, as if a man, to shed tears in abundance into the saint's lap, and so to weep, frothing greatly.

Which when the attendant saw, he began to drive away that weeping mourner; but the saint forbade him, saying: "Let him alone! As he loves me so, let him alone; that into this my bosom he may pour out the tears of his most bitter lamentation. Behold! thou, even seeing that thou art a man, and hast a rational soul, couldst in no way know anything about my departure, except what I myself have lately shown to thee; but to this brute animal, destitute of reason, in what way soever the Maker Himself hath willed, He hath revealed that his master is about to go away from him."

And, so saying, he blessed his sorrowing

servant the horse, then turning about to go away from him.

And going forth thence, he ascended the little hill that overlooks the monastery, and stood for a little while on the top of it, and, standing with both hands lifted up, he blessed the monastery, saying: "To this place, small and mean though it be, not only the Scotic kings (Irish and Dalriadic) with their peoples, but also the rulers of strange and foreign nations, with the people subject to them, shall bring great and extraordinary honour; by the saints also of other churches shall no common reverence be shown."

After these words, descending from that little hill, and returning to the monastery, he sat in his cell transcribing the Psalter; and coming to that verse of the Psalm where it is written, *But they who seek the Lord shall want no manner of thing that is good,* "Here," he says, "at the end of the page, I must cease. What follows let Baithene write."

The last verse which he had written was very suitable for the saint at his departure, to whom eternal things that are good shall never be wanting; while the following verse was most suitable for his successor, as a father and teacher of spiritual sons: *Come, ye children, and hearken*

unto me; I will teach you the fear of the Lord. And
indeed he, as his predecessor enjoined, succeeded him not only in teaching, but also in
transcribing.

After the transcription of the aforesaid verse,
at the end of the page, the saint enters the church
for the evening Vespers of the Lord's Day vigil,
and as soon as this is over he returns to his cell,
where he had bare rock for his bedding, and a
stone for his pillow, which to this very day is
standing by his grave as a kind of sepulchral
monument; and he sits on the bed through the
night.

And so, there sitting, he gives his last commands to the brethren, in the hearing of his
attendant only, saying: "These last words, O
my children, I commend unto you; that ye have
mutual   and   unfeigned   charity   among
yourselves, with peace. And if, according to the
example of the holy fathers, ye shall attend to
this, God, the Comforter of good men, will help
you; and I, abiding with Him, will intercede for
you. And not only shall the necessaries of this
present life be sufficiently supplied by Him, but
He will also bestow those rewards of eternal
riches, which are laid up for them that keep His
divine laws."

Thus far we have drawn up, recounted in a short paragraph, the last words of our venerable patron, spoken just as he was passing over from this weary pilgrimage unto the heavenly country.

After which, as his happy last hour gradually approached, the saint was silent. Then, in the middle of the night, at the sound of the ringing of the bell, he rises in haste and goes to the church; and, running more quickly than the rest, he enters alone, and on bended knees falls down in prayer beside the altar.

Diormit his attendant, following more slowly, at the same moment sees from a distance that the whole church is filled within, in the direction of the saint, with angelic light. But when he approaches the door, the same light that he had seen, which was also seen by a few other of the brethren, as they were standing at a distance, quickly disappeared.

So Diormit, entering the church, keeps on asking, in a lamentable voice: "Where art thou, Father?" And, feeling his way through the darkness, the lights of the brethren not yet being brought in, he finds the saint prostrate before the altar; and, lifting him up a little and sitting beside him, placed the holy head in his bosom.

And meanwhile, the congregation of monks running up with the lights and seeing their father dying, began to weep. And, as we have learnt from some who were there present, the saint, his soul not yet departing, with his eyes opened upward, looked about on either hand with a wonderful cheerfulness and joy of countenance; doubtless seeing the holy angels coming to meet him.

Then Diormit lifts up the holy right hand of the saint that he may bless the choir of monks. But also the venerable man himself, so far as he could, at the same time moved his hand, so that he might still be seen, while passing away, to bless the brethren by the motion of his hand, though he was not able to do so with his voice. And, after his holy benediction thus expressed, he immediately breathed out his spirit. Which having left the tabernacle of the body, his face remained ruddy, and wonderfully gladdened by an angelic vision; so that it appeared not to be that of one dead, but of one living and sleeping. Meanwhile the whole church resounded with mournful lamentations.

But there is a thing which seems not one to be passed over, which was revealed to a certain saint of Ireland at the same hour in which his

blessed soul departed. For in that monastery
which in the Scotic (Irish) tongue is named
Cloni-finchoil (Rosnarea?) there was a certain
holy man, an aged soldier of Christ, just and
wise, who was named Lugud son of Tailchan.

Now this man early in the morning, with
many sighs, related his vision to one who was,
equally with himself, a Christian soldier, Fergno
by name; saying: "In the middle of this last
night, the holy Columba, the pillar of many
churches, passed away to the Lord. And in the
hour of his blessed departure, I saw in the spirit
the whole of Iona, to which I have never come
in the body, irradiated by the brightness of
angels, and the whole space of the air up to the
ethereal regions of the heavens illumined by the
brightness of the same angels, who, sent from
heaven, descended in countless numbers to bear
away his holy soul. High-sounding strains also,
and very sweet songs of the angelic hosts, did I
hear in the very moment of the departure of his
holy soul among the angelic choirs ascending up
on high."…

Meanwhile, after the departure of his holy soul,
the hymns for the morning being ended, the
sacred body is carried back, with the tuneful

psalmody of the brethren, from the church to the cell from which a little before he had come alive. And for three days and as many nights his august obsequies are celebrated with all due honour and ceremonial. And these being ended in the sweet praises of God, the venerable body of our holy and blessed patron, wrapped in clean linen cloths and placed in a coffin that was prepared for it, is buried with due reverence, to rise again in luminous and eternal brightness.

Adamnan's conclusion

After reading these three little books, let each diligent reader note well of how great and of what manner of merit was our holy and venerable abbot, so often mentioned above; of how great and of what manner of honour he was esteemed in the sight of God; how great and on what manner were those angelical and luminous visits to himself; how great was the grace of prophecy that was in him; how great the efficacy of divine virtues; how great and how frequent the brightness of divine light that shone around him while yet abiding in this mortal flesh; which same celestial brightness, even after the departure of his most kindly soul from the tabernacle of the body, does not cease to shine around the place in which his sacred bones rest; where also there is a frequent visitation of angels, as is considered proved, being shown to certain chosen persons.

And this extraordinary favour has also been conferred by God on the same man of blessed memory, by which, though he lived in this small and remote island of the British sea, his name has merited to be honourably noised abroad, not only throughout the whole of our own Scotia, and Britain, the greatest of all the islands of the whole world; but to reach even as far as three-cornered Spain, and the Gauls, and Italy, which lies beyond the Pennine Alps, yea, even to the city of Rome itself, which is the head of all cities. So great and such notable honour is known, among other marks of divine favour, to have been conferred on the same saint by God, Who loves them that love Him, and, more and more glorifying those who magnify Him with sweet praises, lifts them up on high with immeasurable honours, Who is blessed for ever. Amen.

I beseech those, whoever they may be, that wish to transcribe these books, yea rather, I adjure them by Christ the Judge of the worlds, that after they have diligently transcribed, they will collate and correct them with all care, according to the copy from which they have written, and also subscribe this adjuration in its place:

Whosoever reads these books of the virtues of Columba, let him pray God for me, Dorbhene, that I may possess eternal life after death.